A Burning Lake of Paper Suns

J.D.

Thank you so much for all the
stars you make language. Always
live deliciously. ☺

—Ellen
Welcker

A Burning Lake of Paper Suns

poems by Ellen Webre

MOON
TIDE PRESS

~ 2021 ~

A Burning Lake of Paper Suns
© Copyright 2021 Ellen Webre

Editor-in-chief
Eric Morago

Editor Emeritus
Michael Miller

Marketing Specialist
Ellen Webre

Proofreader
Jim Hoggatt

Front cover art
Amanda Le

Book design
Michael Wada

Moon Tide logo design
Abraham Gomez

A Burning Lake of Paper Suns
is published by Moon Tide Press

Moon Tide Press
6709 Washington Ave. #9297
Whittier, CA 90608
www.moontidepress.com

FIRST EDITION

Printed in the United States of America

ISBN # 978-1-7350378-7-5

For everyone I have ever loved, and for everyone who has loved me.

Contents

Foreword

If Simone Weil's assertion that "The truly precious things are those forming ladders reaching towards the beauty of the world, opening onto it" is true, then Ellen Webre's thorn-studded stanzas build a scaffolding to carry the reader through aching need until they are ready to open themself to the dark beauty of life. I first became aware of Webre close to a decade ago—still in college, she was already an established member of the Southern California poetry community. Coming across as thoughtful and demure, even then her poetic voice was vivid, feral, and unique. I realized early on that Ellen Webre was a woman determined to stay complex. I have looked forward to this book ever since I first heard her perform.

In Webre's rich language, the world breaks. It splits like overripe fruit, filling the page with heady wine-scented poems. She takes a personal, intimate feeling and expands it to the mythical, writing a new and truly precious folklore to live in. She is an oracle of the unknowable. As a wild witch of language, Webre deftly weaves the senses together; filling your hands with a dark loom, sliding the spectre of fruit and raw flesh across your tongue, and surrounding you with forest and snow until you are a creature of magic. But in this primal tapestry, there runs the threads of compellingly relatable human nature.

There is comfort in separating yourself from pain. It becomes easy to speak dispassionately and divorce oneself in the darkest of fears and impulses. Webre leans in. She turns her desires into a feast, feeds us on her poems piled onto a silver platter heavy laden with pomegranates and allegory. With all her saturate imagery, Webre's mind swims through mythology and magic with ephemeral grace; we follow in her wake. In the end, the power of these poems is not about how much magic Webre can reveal for us; the power is in how the mystical, sometimes dark, sometimes glorious, can show us ourselves. As Wittgenstein declared "We are asleep. Our Life is a dream. But we wake up sometimes, just enough to know that we are dreaming."

—HanaLena Fennel

Ashes

After "Confetti" by Sheila J Sadr

Let there fly a dark confetti,
charcoal dusted with constellations.
Let them fall into the ocean.
Into the bayou. Let them sodden
into lotus tongues, orchid mouths,
spiced gingeroot's twisting body.
Crushed blackberries.
Black garlic to dye skin purple,
let it be as honeyfinger bee stings
when touched, raising mountains
where the blood dances arterial.
Let them smell of burnt ghost,
oh candle wax, oh Spanish rosemary.
Grave dirt made incense
for the right sting of lungs.
They are shaken from my hair,
these petaled gnats,
that have nested in the hollow
of my skullcap. Do you dare
stand spider-laced in my bite?
Open-mouthed to my ashes
flaking pale as bone?
You, my golden jasmine,
my night-blooming amber,
will you become the soil
of my wild almonds?
Will you hold their pulpy masses
together until it beats again,
a fist-sized heart
hissing like a cat?

I

Origin Story

It was like this,

                          innocence,

           traded

      for the knowledge

       of old age

              sickness

                and death.

That   tart apple of contemplation,

          the sugar fruit which dims

               the spark

                   of paradise,

casting children

             in exile

      from the shallows,

        I,   a tongue-tied little monster.

             I,   a lonely king

devouring worlds in a day

    was someone to be reckoned with

           in potential.

    Oh how valiantly

      I scoffed at boys

         on the playground,

   the girls

      and their dolls,

when my fields

     were full of warriors

            and my puppets

    the theaters of intrigue

      and dark sorcery.

I couldn't do a push-up   if I tried,
        flinched from the ball,
                the bat,
the intellectual mundanity,
        of *tag.*

        Instead, I imagined
                a red-stringed love   of past lifetimes
                        some long-haired poet
                whose slender fingers
                        could pluck the stars
                from the sky.

So, I built myself
        a house of firs,
gathered ferns
        and firewood,
shared a flameless hearth
        with the wind   and rabbits
                behind the school.

        There,
        I feasted
        on dandelions
                like ambrosia

with only ghosts
                to witness

                what I longed for.

Teenagers Will Scream if You Love Them

We children of dark horses, the silver-tongued and claw-tipped,
the furry-tailed and horned gods of transport cry
and christen this car as holy chariot. We children of carved tools
press our knees to leather, smack boots to rubber road,
our hands and lips in prayer for hangdog mouths burbling
the holy wine of bones and beginning. We break the bread
of dreams in milk teeth, hungry for divine spit and circumstance.
Here we howl, here we ride in the belly of the morning
and evening sun. The world wakes to our shrieking
for the pleasure of our king, oh blue-eyed, oh ripped jeans
and perfect knees, he wears a coronet of thorns sideways,
smoking cloves and clover, burning us charcoal. We spread our skin
for the rip of his carnelian clutch, when he takes our throats tender,
sows seeds of black bruising, sweet violet.
We shake off sleep like dogs in water, we ribbon fingers in gold
to whip trains raw, we light cigarettes with explosions,
you've never seen anything like this before, new girl,
open wide and swallow a golden yolk, soft sacrament
falling from His hands. Our King thinks you deserve
a taste of the future. Child, come crawling or we shall drag you
in crooked, scraping your knees in the supplication you crave
whenever he strikes the concrete. Your smoke rises
at every graze of his holy. He could scrimshaw your bones
right out of your body, rope your ankles and flay you slow.
You would still blush scarlet; you would still sing his name.
He knows, you know. Can't help but smile out the window
at the scorched earth we have razed in his honor. Can't speak,
can't say what he wants without making it true. You bring out
the ocean in him, the sweat stuttering stammer of soft shaking
in his sacrilege, the way his hands flex from the branding
your hands give. Teenagers will scream if you love them,
so give him a kiss, girlie, summon your courage.
You'll hear his voice through us, our never-ending wail.

My Closed-Circuit Songs, Frail Ground Without Exit

There is a light beneath my eyelids.
There is a lantern in my stomach.
    I burn from a hundred angles,
        but like a fish
    shadowed in ice,
my lips, half frozen,
        my eyes, glass mirrors,
   are mouthing imitations
   of amorous intent.

I Want to Be the Queen of Air and Darkness

After Elliot Fried

I want to recline on a silken couch,
sipping cider from a skull cap.

I want three raven familiars to preen at my shoulder
and lounge forebodingly over my doorway.

I want my witch boys smooth as smoke
nibbling blackcurrants from my ringed fingers.

And towers. And storm clouds.
And a black velvet aesthetic with spiders.

I want to be legendary,
to match wits with heroes who bang

at my door with the zeal of God's angels
to lay me down.

I want a scorpion's kiss.
I want a crown of steel.

I want the moon,
the moon,

and to feel like I am home
in my own body.

Little Hunger

I waited all through the night   to hear him speak,

     devoured   his shimmering, sipped

at his words   like black milk   and holy water,

     I fed on his gurgling throat,   took my fill

of his cadaver,   for I had been   empty

     of experience   and I thirsted

for raw organs.   He split his skull and no lover

     could have been richer.   For this

I traded   my first beating heart,   for this

     I traded my last   working mind.

My flesh for his flesh,   my skin for his skin,

     one body knitted together   so long as he stayed

in my stomach,   so long   as I could gnaw

     and lick and chew   and swallow.

The Voyeur

Quiet,   from the other room, I watch you
      liquify, to brown butter,
         to syrup.
I watch
      your throat bloom
               with asphodel,
     daffodil,
                 bullet wound,
       your breath,
                    such breath.

I desire
      the scythes of your nails,
                your feast of moans,
        the throbbing songs,
   of this pelvic glide,
        like a wine-dark jaguar

           with a plum,
              with a knife.

To Be on the Other Side

in the beginning
        you wrote the answer

                and my body

            burrowed
    into mudflats

                and the pools

        of my eyes
                    charcoaled

            my mouth

            sorrowing
    in the silence

            of the drowned

it was this
        I had been waiting for

                            a portrait

                    of the monster
    I was to become

            your kiss

                made my mouth
                    a bottle-green lake

    your touch

                planted sweetgrass
                    down my spine

I never want
to treat you badly

I want

to make you
feel seen

and heard

so come home to me

let me drink
your dark waters

I have hollowed out

so much space
for your anguish

your fear

it tastes
so sweet

Ghazal for Unbecoming

After Angel Nafis

If none of your lovers come, dismantle your landscape. Be indiscriminate
with your hours. Become trimethylamine, the fragrance of an inescapable girl,

then erase your speech. Bury yourself south until you are root cock legs,
a buried corm, a botanical split along the bedrock, you vegetative girl.

Kill the clarity on the window and suspect the rivers of your infamy. Taper
the sun's entrails around your spangled carpels, just like another dead girl.

When you arrive, keep going, gain hate. Even this poison is an ecstasy.
Let this inflorescence be a rapture when you lay eggs in the carcass of a girl.

Unlearn what the corpse flower forgets. Spathe by spadix, each living grave
becomes a blasphemy of strangers, of carrion beetles, the truth of a flesh-fly girl.

The baddest bliss is a junkyard garden where you were born bleeding. Devil,
cut this breath, wither the stalk, release the ghost, the colony, the stench, the girl.

Dodging the Bullet

All your moonlight has poured
        from mind   to tongue.
           You've twisted,
    and bent your stomach
               over an armrest
               for hours
        just to hold his hands.

You took the seat
           with a broken belt
      so that he would be safe, but

he says

      There is nothing in you.

There is nothing in you,
        and I am tired
            of pretending
               to care.

      You suddenly realize   your enrollment
           with him in the school
               of heartbreak
where poets learn
           of their longings,   the craft,
               the nightmares of being

in a carnivorous feast,
           in the mortifying ordeal

    of being unknown.

So, I Went into Exile

I.
Because I lay naked in a dorm room
without the benefit of the dark,
a gilded snake, drunk
on the cascade of your body,
sucking the marrow
out of each boiled bone.

II.
Because I was half-starved.
Because I knew nothing else before this.

III.
Because the world never found the whys
of my carelessness, misnaming my devotion
with the doubt I filleted from my ribs
to feed you, whom I fed from.

Here, take my time, each folded decade of growth
I have no use for without your secrets.

IV.
Because I was there. And heavy, and terrible.
You called me empty for the way I hung
pendulous on your every mouthful of distraction,
whatever story you used to keep me
from bearing witness to what you lacked.

V.
Because you had no tourniquet
to staunch the ambitions I drained
from your skin. Parched
in the hours of a wind-blown desert.

An Alternate History of First Love

I have my whimpered way with his hands,
      his endless mouth,   and I leave.
            Before sunrise.
     Before he deceives me
        with an overflow
     I mistake
          for divine honesty.

In this one, I refuse   the charcuterie of his grief,
               his yearnings,
     his way of rooting out
         the sad girl   in every monstress.

This time,
       I play *him* like a fiddle,   make *him* scream
         when I perform
           the mad girlfriend
      he's always wanted
             to pull back
               from the edge

I am the untethered giggle of flame
      at the curtains,   the gas tank,
         licking at his throat
           with a sizzling brand
              of *mine, mine*
and he will cry out my name
        as only a sad boy can.

     Here, I am not in love.
        I am not patient or kind.
I do not lose my voice   to his.
         I do not think   I can see
            what no one else does,

        and I do not want
    to make him feel whole.

3 A.M. in a Yellow Basement

For a moment,   the Three of Swords
    is slipped
        from the banter
            of my missing ribs,
suspended,
    a graduation card
        telling bitter truths
            to no one,

On this night,   the world hobbles
        its gaze
    into a white river,
           diaphanous
    from horizon to horizon,

and I   am scented with dust
                and olives,
        and we
            are cuddled
in beanbags,
    speaking
        through the little hours,
soundtracked
    by the snoring
        of another man's liquor.

I draw my arm
    around the kindness   of a boy
        I will never see again.

I bury myself
    in the crook of his shoulder,
                my cheek
    surfing the rhythm
        of a foreign heartbeat.

We lift our vulnerabilities
                    to lamplight,
        drinking from glasses
            of sangría.

Even now I can taste
                    the grapes
        of this summer ghost,
                    the kissed eyelids
I carry into every battle
                        like a talisman.

The End of Dreaming

After Ada Limón

Enough of the rabbit,
the trembling, the fucking,
wide-eyed tender of burrowed den.
Enough of the fox, her cunning,
the foolish farmer and his cart of fish,
the bear who breaks his tail in the ice.
No more firebirds,
the turmeric smears on teacups,
pollen and honeysuckle,
enough of faltering hands,
peace, and lilac-heavy lungs
wheezing their last.

I want to be uncomfortable.
To feel the heat of our almost-touch,
the nuzzle of nose to cheek,
arched back stretch
of something real and writhing.
The taste of blood and soil,
of moss and petrichor, of
clean sheets and warm bodies
snuggled against the winter.

I want an end to dreaming
of flying ships and talking cats,
of Koschei the Deathless and Baba Yaga.
Give me stars and skeletons if you must,
but give me your hand first,
your punk-fisted mouth,
the way you hold me
like you could carry me forever,
the way I want to carry you.

Always.
        Always.

II

Into My Arms

Out of my dreams,   you arrive
        like a burning lake
                of paper suns

With you, I am
        violet and gold,
                flickering,
a dandelion
        basking in the sun-drench
                of another curling midnight.

This easy exchange
                of bloodstreams,
        this friendship
                and ecstasy,
this orbiting of the moon
                        is a dance
                of mandarin ducks.

You,   my peridot,
                sage fire, you,
        crest the hills
                of purification,

and with trembling hands, I salute
        my approaching paradise,
                breathing in
        the perfumed verses
                of our sudden
        but natural
                intimacies.

The Budding Boy

After the painting "Budding Boy" by Julie Heffernan

White limbed and long, a scattering of bones and moonlight
      twined with sinew and red hair.

He stands barefoot, naked as the tree he has grown from,
      holds the bounty he has gathered

to his stomach: peaches, pomegranates, blackberries, and bird skulls,
      these eggshells of what he is made of.

I find him outside my window after a night of uprooted sheets.
      He looks back like a cherry blossom

floating away on a river of mercury. Oh, he is the salt and rice of me,
      my sighs by honeyed candleburn,

an apple that calls with the hiss of a snake, coaxes a meeting
      of tongue and lips like prayers.

His fingers dig into the branches, searching for steadiness, waiting
      for my mouth to swallow

the whole of him, the nectar of his blooming, white petals
      in their unraveling.

The Pink Light

The night you held my hand

                                         the night

    caressed my palms   my hollow hips

held me safe   in the light

              & I danced   openly

with your hands I fell   without looking

    & the pink   dancing

        on our fingers

        on your skin

    when you   held my hand

     & I   didn't look

         & you

    caressed my lips

     & I was falling

       & the night

was a night   I belonged in

      our sudden kiss forever

in the pink light we shared a dance   of hands

   & holding

of wolves & rabbits

              & stars   & safe

maybe I need   I need this

             falling

& your skin   is mine   I said

             my stars you said

                    the night

Almond Blossom

I have spent a thousand years
picking myself   out of the middle of nowhere

on an empty highway   clutching fistfuls
of fireflies to my eyes   clawing poppy

blossoms across a belly   full of rabbits
    I dripped with peppercorns   I salted

the earth   as if that would make   the mud
easier to swallow   I buried the creatures

with a pocket watch   and a dead fish
and mounds rose up   the hills   of my body

a congregation of sparrows   sang like nightingales
    as if that would bring me peace   my ghost

is mad Ophelia babbling   in swampflower
poltergeisting the highways   and waiting

for the next thud   of wooden dolls   slapped
out of my hands   brings me walnut shells

to curl into   like that could keep me safe
from waking up   again   in the cheekbone curve

of a boy   who does not know the difference
between a raven and a writing desk   between

I'm sorry   and   have some wild almonds,
love   I picked these myself

you'll have to kiss me   to taste them

Helpless

But even now I

          am not afraid,

Though perhaps   there is reason

    to be afraid of me,

for I have worn stag skulls   splintered

        over my honesty

with foxgloves   dripping

    down each twisted antler,

        the nectar sap

        of poisoned raspberries.

But he reaches for me   anyway,

    as if I wasn't   sinew and fat,

smouldering in the pyre,

    as if the blue flames

        of Tartarus

      hadn't already   picked its way

across my two

        black oceans.

Clean
Inspired by Bloodbourne

The boy nuzzles the peach curve of me
from my kitchen floor after feasting
on a midday meal of curry and ginger brew.

My hands are tied in this way, bound
in soap and sponge to kitchen sink,
to little hours before work
while the wet flick of worship circles
shellfulls of dark honey in the daytime.

I speak of doll and doctor
weaving the beasts of nightmares
with nimble fingers. When Secrets beckoned
sweetly, she cut her throat for an honest end.
A corpse should be left well enough alone.
Mania makes mothers of the dead.

Still the boy laps at my shoreline,
nestled in my most unknown country.
Had I the hands to sculpt a lifeless thing,
I would immortalize him too.

As deftly as I wash what remains of our hunger,
as deftly as he cleans the drippings of dessert.

In the Bone Pit

Oh mine, oh mine
    this entrance,   and exit,

    my river   of oil,
my river of blood

    I've scrimshawed   my pelvis
        with your name

    and no one else
        shall scream it   again.

    My silk,   my starling
I am twisted and terrible

                  in these sheets,
    broken back tender   and

      coiled   in wire
                  hold me

    and I shall become
            gardenia sweet. Forgive me

my bitter herbs, wormwood
    milk thistle   and I shall kneel

    before   your needled
          knee caps   press open mouth

          to every hollow, suckling
    the elixirs of your galaxies   dry.

You Make the World Quiet, He Said

And in this,   I am an invention,
      the truth,
           the eater of light
               and sound
to such a degree
      that there is no world
            beyond this bed,
      no bodies in the streets,
      no seas of hunger
           on every wild
                streetcorner.
    I am safe.
           I am the stillness
              of shuttered windows,
and nails inscribing
           calligraphy
      across dunes of skin.

He calls me a shepherd,
             a cradler of the moon
              by duskfall.
There is no one else
      left to hear
    the blood rhythm
      of my heartbeat
           against his cheek.
It is our decree
      that no one can stir us,
we nestle of foxes,
           we denned rabbits post-fuck,
    nuzzling away
at the divine melancholy,
        of a collarbone's
           kissed shoreline.

Of Moss and Kerosene

I have not mastered the art of compassion
through violence. The only blood I know
is that which weeps through the slit of my undoing.

Here marks a hollow grave
where my blessed un-children, my clots
of garnet wisp an iron river out of this body.

But you, raging to crunch of bone
of cartilage, of fenders in detachment,
the unzipping of skin by carmine blade,

by razor whip of scarlet sand, you
defender of the trembling, Valkyrie
with a dark throat and moth wings,

I know what flecks your knuckles—
have sucked at the ruin beneath your nails,
a doll on fire, a howling moon. Witness me,

making love to the beastly strength
of your slender wrists, I know you as justice,
my gathering of violets, my silvered mouth.

Oh Molotov rebel, kerosene-guzzling war boy,
I do not have the tenderness to unleash my rage
like carnivorous moss upon the vile.

I hold nothing but what weeps a miscarriage
of famine, but you are my ever drink of water.
You are the green place of my Valhalla.

Adonis, with Blackened Field

It is easier to dig   in the springtime
    to root in loam rich   as raspberries,
to bloom,   to harvest where your hands
    have nourished my wild thirsts.   I bead
with cherry sap, I drip the nectar
    of libation wine.   Boy,   you feed me
blackcurrants from thickets,   cider from gilded pears
    you've picked by the armful.

You delight my songbirds   and I have had you
    in every way a god can,   except
in supplication. So I kneel,
    and am abruptly alone with burnt grass,
seized in the salt and smoke   of first wound,
    first shrapnel jab of bronze blade,
the swollen want   that made me
    the unhollow dog   of a deceiver.

I bury my knuckles   where my virgin body lies,
    an unfinished wolf,   slurring blood
in the grip   of open palms,   dry as bone
    unsatisfied,   unyielding with gritted teeth,
bearing the breaking shift   of shoveled earth.
    With you I'd forgotten   what it was to buckle
under the weight   of a gardener whose attention
    would not steward   the land he tilled.

Broken ivory,   hanks of hair,   pomegranates
    and corpses   peeling like paper gloves.
Here, is the fault,   the chasm,   my devoured skin
    in a bed of cinders.   Turn me around   boy
give me your   uncracked cavities   of sky,
    your birth,   your death
unraveling where our hips meet,   where you writhe
    like a viper,   hissing my name.

Mine

In a famous gallery

of photographs

you are enormous.

Three stories,   of naked moonlight

glistening slick   with coconut oil,

bathed,   and

beaded in rosewater

reclining,

blue eyes lit

by candle

burning

on blackened fingertips,

smears of crushed

poppies

on your chest,   my bite marks

on your neck,

purpled violets

sprouting from the cream.

How soft,

bound in silk cord

to a banyan tree,   peach

blossoms

tumbling down

your shoulders   like wine,

Snakes curl

up your calves
as if you

were the golden apple

of Hesperides,

of knowledge,

of sin.

Here in the snow,   bare as the trees,

you hold a skull

to   clay-cold lips.

Know that it is

my face

in your hands,

that it is   my kiss

and breath   and heart

you steal

each time I take a picture.

A picture.

With which I claim your soul

from the angels.

With which I display you.

An Omen of Damascus Steel

After Brendan Constantine

It starts
with an unfinished blade,
hilt set with emerald
and citrine.

It makes a claim
on the celestial,
on the broken
petaled tulip
one lover
offers another.

It mentions   something
about
an irreversible choice,
the joyous collision
of a girl and
an oncoming train,
both singing
an owl song
into
red water.

But   as the dusk
falls
it captures
the reflection
of uncertainty
perched
in the shrubbery,
a heart
a target

murmuring
secret doubts.

Don't Look Down

You head toward a life you won't be living.

— Kim Hyesoon

The hand in your hand is already a ghost.

What you don't know keeps you running
on air after the cliff gives way.

Confession: there is no truth that will keep
you and your joy in the same sky.

The ghost in your hand is flickering,
begging, drowning. Do you know?

Your joy is crying, is overwhelmed.
Your joy is taking off his face.

Don't look down.

He is still behind you. But you do not see him.
He is waving goodbye. But you do not turn.

You hold your hands and head toward a life
you won't be living because all you believe in

is the indigo night of a future
you will never get to hold. Because

your muscles are made of prayer,
and gravity knows your worth.

Fruit of the Buried

Neither a mouthful of coins nor a sea
                              of elegies
          will pay passage
                    from the dark.

Unstitch your wired lips
          and let them spill
                    onto the floor
     of the cathedrals crumbling
                         in your heart.

Soon, you will meet the threshold
          of all you've stolen.

                    Your very life,
          a burgundy pitch staircase
                    carved of spruce and bone.
          Do not look back.

Do not look back.
               Shed your silks,
          and silver talismans.
               Shed the blood clot songs
          of your bursting
                         body.

Now you are free,
               and it is in your eyes
          where black figs bloom.

It is in your tears
          where wasps
                    are born
               in splendor and abyss.

Take my hand, let me taste
                    with fiery tongue
          the anointed skin
                    and pulp

of your sweetness,

This feast, as endless as absence.
This feast, my blessed devouring.

III

Portrait of the Day After My 24th Birthday

After Chen Chen

With your father's book.
Without your promised chili.
With broken ground beneath my feet.
Without, even now, an appetite.
With stifled tears. At the diner, and at the grocery store.
With my father saying *you shouldn't have been serious*
until it was serious. Without the moon. Without my body.
With a prosthetic mouth. With your text
and the film shoot where I received the text.
With praying that I would be unbroken by this.
Because when we met,
the road before me alchemized,
a restoration of ruined harbors.
Perhaps I can go on,
with or without you.

The Failings of Joy

a destructive force of wanting

                    dashing itself on the rocks

there lies Joy glinting with salt

                    and floating on crested waves

look how she dissipates

                    as rose petals do when drunk

look at how she draws a name

                    across a gunmetal sea

away from my streaming hair

                    when the night drapes herself

over the horizon

                    only her stars will know what rapid

thrills

once echoed in my pulse

                    shook to unraveling

for a trembling name

                    for a wolf howl and shriek

that only loss knows

                    in silence

The City That Love Built

The city that love built rests upon a hill.
That is to say,   it looks like death
from a distance,
splintered skull fragments
piercing up from a crater
the size of a fist,
of a heart,
of a world
smashing into another world.
It is a crown of ivory and red canals,
it has been there since the first sweetness,
the first weeping.

It is its own five-fingered cage.
If you listen
you can hear how it breathes,
how it makes you home on every street,
in every alley and flophouse,
in every prison and palace.

If you taste its lemon candy, its old chocolate,
you will be disappointed
by the way it sours,
turns bitter in your teeth.

When you crystal-tongue moon sugar,
lift spiced-honey fingers to your lips,
you will sorrow
that there is no more
and never will be again.

Drown in peach nectar instead,
know that you cannot bring yourself
to swallow it all,
even though you are hummingbird hungry,
even though it deserves to be drunk.

Find yourself alone in a courtyard full of birds
        holding keys to buildings
                you cannot enter,
        where people you cannot save   go hungry
                        and will not leave—
                        don't even want to,
        no matter how patiently you wait at their door.

You knock at their windows,
        you beg them to get some fresh air,
                but they ignore you,
        writing their guilt on the walls
                slipping the occasional thank you note
                        or confession,
        telling you to get some sleep,
                                to just leave,
in code you choose to ignore
        until they stop trying.

You don't know if they were really there
                to begin with,
        if it was all in your head
                and you have nothing
                        to give anyone.

If you did, no one would want it
                        anyway.

Waiting with Insomnia

Neither bloodhound

    nor rabbit

  has ears as sharp

    as the ones I use

to listen for your clicking bones.

You used to snap apple branches

  at your clawing,

    we brewed mead

from the nectar

  of your footfalls.

We were drunk all autumn long,

  but now neither gauntlet

    thrown at gravestone

nor my desperate decrees

  summon ghosts.

Instead, only the platitudes

  of your sliced-tongue supplicants

    kiss the crowns

  of your hips,

which were once my roast hart

                for the feasting.

In this exile,

      neither canary song

           nor burrowed snakes

can soften the frost

      of each shrieking star

           you crystalize

on knifed fingertips

      of absence.

I am displaced,

      at the curb

where we once shared milk tea,

      reenacting with my shadow

the ritual sacrifice

      of our first kiss.

Ten Months Later

I am in a car and crying and confessing
again, left behind, smoked and stolen
by moonlight, still groveling
down the gasoline trail of my devotions.

The distant piper mocks me
with their strange nakedness, their leaving,
disdainful, self-loathing, letting me go
for my own good—never mind
that I'll pick laments from my teeth
for years, never mind that they've plucked
every star out of the sky.

Emptiness puts on weight in my throat.
I find that I cannot speak
for a vertigo of fever, for the red mirrors
I drip on the driver's seat
where my lover has carved
a golden war across your arms.

There Are Women Who Hold Skulls

There are women who hold skulls
        like the children they cannot carry,

        clamping chatter-teeth ivory
around strangleholds of neck and breast,

murmuring out the wild moans of forest
        deer in wolf jaw.

        There are women who slide fingers
through eye sockets,

drink wine from skull caps,
        swishing blood in round circles.

        They take their feasts in tents,
on rugs of fur, gold rings on every finger.

These are black-nailed daughters
        of sirens moved inland, where lounges

        fill with the pomegranate-smoke
of their breathing. These are the knife-fight

fools of the alleyways,
        the crystal-globe diviners, the coldhearted

        kick and cackles of the nighttime.
There are women who hold skulls

of the children who failed to be born,
        bursting into bloodmuck by moonlight,

        slipping through stained fingers
and pitched into pyres.

Hollow-eyed and paying no debts to sorrow,
   they are never to feel remorse.

   Never to feel hearts
beating double in their bodies.

Monstress

Take me for a flower-

           crowned creature

with sharp teeth   and soft bite,

    some   forked tongue   siren

          who has lost her tact.

It is 3 AM and I

        am making confession

                  to one

    who thinks me a liar,

or at least   doesn't believe

    what I say I mean.

               And it is wise.

       And it is the truth.

I have been lying

                  in wait.

      In alleys

        and cellars

trying to make myself

a home

    for any   broken-hearted boy

       foolish enough

               to crawl inside.

   Yet he is

               A teasing little shit.

       Exposing   heart-strings

on the cutting board,

        testing my addiction

             without offering a morsel.

It sends my nerves to war

        to be exiled

          in times of peace

     when my   unhinged jaw   opens

             to the ground

      empty.

I Know How It Feels to Be Big

After Jeremy Ra

Wheezing through a carapace

                    I've punctured with a corkscrew

       to make my lungs

              collapse faster

everything is excess

              it is boring

                        to wave these hands of gold

          at every stranger

     who lights

              a cigarette on the gas stove

                        of my belly

I just want to be dormant

          cold

              abalone

                        but

there are so many oceans

          sloshing between my ears

              too many surfers

                        cresting its ink

       and saliva

          only to drown at base of my throat

                      clog up the drain

so that I am doubly speechless

          stuffed to the gills with coins

                  people slot through my lips

like I could grant wishes

          or spit money

I'd rather be a wolf,

                     a flounder
            no one would bother with
                                      if they had the
choice
but they always do

                                    it kills me to be this
famous

           catering to the rabble
                         too discontented to luxuriate
    in the drought
                 they build

                 of my body

Ekphrastic of the Wicked

I play with fire. Flip black petals
between my fingers, papered nightshades
of my withered pulsing. Here I am,
reckless, like the tarot card Fool
with smiling eyes and hidden mouth,
furiously prognosticating against being whole.

Green as greed, I have spilled
formaldehyde of pickled memory
through my stitched lips, tombstone teeth.
Conceal them in a place where so many
moonflowers have become salt and ash,
lest I beg to sign my life over to bones

again and again and again in the
gold script of my relentless blood.

Scientists Estimate There Are 400 Billion Stars No One Loves

They're wrong of course.
                     But scientists
             have yet to master
                           communication
                 between earth and
        the celestial menagerie.

If there are   at least 400 billion stars
           they do not account for,
                  it is because
             they don't know your address.
         Or that California burns a moat
                 of flame to keep you safe.

Beloved,
            if I were made
               of gentler wheat,
           I would have given you
              the last bread
                 of my body.
       Let you sink teeth
             in the spice
        of this tender throat, but
      I can offer you nothing
you haven't already
     swallowed.

How casually then
                you gnaw at
      the pomegranate pulp
        of my gristle,
            so very like an apple
    you plucked from a snake
        like desire.

Field Notes on the Body

1.

I wear this painted skin
            like a nightgown
        in a flattened plain.

            I bear its billowing,
                    flaking into stars.

Sometimes I hear my shoulders whisper
                    about the way
        my body denies itself,

                    struggles me out
of my own tendons

            in uncaring ruptures
                        of skin
            so that only a skeleton

                        stands stilted
                            beside it.

2.

I dreamed of cutting myself open once,
        my belly distending
            with handprints
                    and aggrieving mouths.

I used kitchen scissors
            and tender saints spilled
        out in teams of trout,
                    gasping
            for a new deprivation,
                    righting the great wrongs
                        of mercy.

3.

I don't know what to value,

 my close-mouthed mornings,

and the scent of cinders.

in this bloating furnace,

of ritual touch?

my blighted eyes,

full of spit

Who could delight

this addict

Just Us and the Void

The dark tasted
                    like rice wine,
          like ghost fire
it's us, echoes of bronze
                    and steel,
the distant laughter
                    of the boneyard.

                    Beneath a butcher's boots,
we are a pair of lamentations.
     We are beyond all questions,
                    spineless
               with our boundaries,
     how empty, how empty,
                              you cry,
     and yes,
               it is a hushed impossibility
that we should ever find a shape
     with which to hold
               each other's hands

                    again.

Exorcism

All fires seem holy if you whisper names
as you light them. My sister, place your candles
in a circle, make mantra of men you would take
between a match and fingertip.

Oh forked-tongue quiet girl, you will flicker
through skins like a shadow, lift quail eggs
to your lips, scrawl prophecy in ink and rosewater.

When the crows come to your windowsill,
offer your handkerchief, and they will peck secrets
across your knuckles, and then the next person
you punch in the face will deserve it.
The next hand you hold will be yours for life.

I give you my marbles, my feral horses,
my crystal skulls, promises of a life
in the Milky Way. You and I will build a fortress
on the moon and dine on nothing but violets
and our bruised enemies.

Those who brave the thorny paths
to our affections will live like kings.
We will glide among them like butterflies,
but until we brush off all the love notes,
we can light this sage. Sit silent
among oleander and smoke
out all his fingerprints from your skin.

IV

The Ladder to the Genitals of God

It's made of black leather,

      salt rope twisted in cognac,

spiced with cherry red drippings:

      salt, brown sugar, dried apricot.

You can pull your fingers from your lips

      and climb to the sliver of light

burning violet on the horizon.

      At the tip is a vanilla pearl,

a mouth dangling a damp

      invitation from the stars.

Red Cento

After Alyssa Matuchniak

summer apples fat-bellied,
by the metal scent of my blood, the silk
nipples dark red,
swollen sugar rubies, dotted
cherry, browning end of harvest: reminder,
of red-paling blossom, deepening
your rich red linen lies,
your crimson ritual of purity, cleansed
in lipstick
like blood, shiny and ruby dark,
flicker of garnet on Persephone's teeth

Verdean Waves

Belts of silver   swing

      around rosy hips,

see how they shift in bangle swirls,

      river shine in its gunmetal blue.

If you seek to lay   your kisses

      in dips   of bone,

warm flesh   soft   invitation,

      take her hands in yours,

lips in pilgrim's prayer.   Lay her down,

      splayed butterfly of burgundy velvet.

Roll down   sheer stockings,

      for she is black sugar,

gold sand   sun-kissed nectar   for your tongue.

Take her gently   by the throat,

      by her curls,   by her hitched

breath   sigh,   and spread the universe   panting   at her feet

      Right here.   Right now.

Old Sorrows

Call me blood of your blood—
pour yourself through me like plum wine.
Let me be the black ink of your calligraphy,
paint me crown to toe with the sutra of our names:
Battlefield Scythe Upon the Wheat,
Pearl on a Dragon's Tongue.

Let your breath fill the hollow
of my bamboo flute body, caress
your fingertips in flight.
We shall out sing the brown nightingale,
the immortal cicada,
and the hungry ghost cry of your house.

Burn the incense, trace my inscription
on the stone. My pulse thrums the red strings
in your hand. Know then that my liver is unwell,
my riverboat glides across a celestial menagerie.

My breath. My bones.

I miss you.

Old Stomping Grounds
After a line by CT Kelly

If you were to return, you would find colossal effigies constructed in your absence.

— CT Kelly

There,   a tall ship in my bathtub, quivering
                            in the surf

There,   the moon in twisted satin, cratered
                             with warm pockets
                                           to nestle in,
                                           safe.

There,   a cup of stars in the kitchen
                            with which I drink my joy.

         I have built you
               into my every minaret
                             of prayer,
with every blade
              I cut my daily meal,
                      with every door
                              that welcomes me home.
Your bones
          are the ribs
                 of my shelter,
Your name,
          imposed so large
              that my devotees
       do not recognize
                 the one
I have sculpted
          into the landscape.

Summer Nights

The cicadas are loudest in August,
when the nights become a short-lived sister
to the buried, when cloying honeysuckle
fills our belly so full dinner
grows cold at the table.

We sit in endless rows of quiet,
twirling ice in our glass just to hear
its melting clink, a season of ghosts,
in the static of a tv screen,
their warm breath exorcising
the toxins of longing,
beading rivulets down the spine
until fabric becomes a painted skin.

If autumn calls, I cannot hear it
over the rats under the floorboards:
the world below, an inverted mirror
where hunger swells
in constellations of fruitfulness.

Dear Matryoshka

I wonder how you keep quiet, a linden wood house of ribs
for the chatter of your own hollow daughters. Is motherhood
truly an eternal bisection, an ancestral cracking
of shells and yolk to be borne and beaten?
I hold my tongue because they sleep often, transfigure themselves
into cats that scent the curves of my ankles.
It seems that I am the sum of these parts, layers of lurking
watchers who yowl, who stretch, and climb into the arms
of whoever will hold them against the crook of their heartbeat,
who listens to the low rumble of their throats,
the soft black music of animals within animals.

Softball Poem
After CT Kelly

You are reaching critical amounts of swing,
your battered heart pitching itself
into the outfield of an empty game.
The ghosts of audience past
thread their fingers in the chain link,
cheers pooling in hollow mouths.

You thank God no one else is here
to watch you scrape your knees
in this blood practice.

You are frightened always and victorious never,
dreading the catch, dreading the run,
yet playing and playing each base.

Sooner or later, you will be good at this.

You will strike your soul into the dark,
let all flying objects be thus devoured,
and no one, no one will stop you
from running home.

The New Year

My distance is already within me,
and it is too late to harken back.
Oil slick spilled in the bathtub,
the rainbow marbled a lace
of water around my hair.

Rosemary is for remembrance,
voices that pressed
their hitched breath,
their quick gasp
against wet tile.

Carve it out,
the sprouting eyes of a potato,
carve out my eyes
which are a symptom of rot.
Peel it. I have no use for skin
that was kissed once,
held another
like a ginger root holds itself.

This is a feast served to the dead,
this is a cold bed in winter,
this is a bloodmouth love I carry
by the scruff of a body
a soul has left behind.

I have traveled too long
and too far. Let it drop
and keep walking.
Like the sun as she dissipates
her fire into the horizon.

Agnostic Poem
After Brendan Constantine

I have made it a habit   not to ask directly
                                          in prayer
      with incense stick,
           prostration,
with pomelos
      and tangerines
           on the altar.

If I whisper into the green light
      in the steps of an escalator,
           what questions of mine can be heard
                by the Emperor of Heaven?

My knowledge of burned wrists
            has made me   wary
                of making demands
                    on the universe,
ere it have me reciprocate
           its gifts beyond
    my means
        of comprehension.

If everything has a price,
           I am afraid to pay it
      though I am a wild spender
              on the credit of my past life.

Is there truly someone,   some system
           keeping score of my

Right Understanding,
Right Intention,
Right Speech,
Right Conduct,
Right Livelihood,
Right Effort,
Right Mindfulness,
Right Samadhi?

And have I done the good work
      in this material land?
Do I dare face my ungrateful self
      that is not a self?

A thousand hands
         with a thousand eyes
have paved the lotuses   I tread upon.

What cup can I drink tea from
         that does not already
have the imprint
      of fate
             on its rim?

Hunter Moon

Space is as thick as sage honey,
swelling up against my palms,
darkness curves around my fingers when I stretch
them across the black milk of the sky.

It is enough for one moment, halting the moon
in her eclipse, through the lunar oils of my skin.
This place on earth, this plateau, are tilled fields
glowing in ridged mounds like rows
of snakeskin inflamed with silver.

I tell my moon that the sky is full of stars, full of graves
hanging on the hooked fingers of some far-off God.
How lasting they are. How small I am,

holding change at bay, stopping the earth from turning
with my *no*. With my *not yet*. Just one moment more,
and somewhere across the world you are sleeping.
You are giving birth. You are falling in love.

I do not know you, but I want you to stay,
to live at least five billion years,
to outlast the ghosts we turn holy by believing.
There is nothing else, yet I am afraid of what is to come:
the universe expanding in us until we return the favor.

Brother Fool

After Marilyn Chin and C.S. Lewis

Brother
you wish to be   a witch's bridegroom
          to clap your hands
                    and let rainbows manacle
                    your wrists
          to the holy rock   of belonging
                                                  but
                    here   on   earth
          your tender heart
          and mind   dance
                              with
                              incompatible
                                        philosophy
                              with sexual   and
                                        literary
                                                  vanity
                    whose heels
                              whet the   blades
                                        of loneliness
                    it scrimshaws   your bones
                              and the blood-veined fingers
                              your family has
                    passed down
                                        for generations

Fool
          if you soak   in a selenite bath   light rose candles
                              paint your horoscope
                                        across your chest
          you will invite
                    crickets into your   bed
                              and their everlasting   croak of dawn
                    will aggravate   the chronic horror
                                        of growing old
                                                  without love
Fool Brother
                    the moon is a confection

                    of rock sugar
    milk wine   screw-taped
                    with anxiety
                    and
                                    uncharitable
                                    impatience for triflers
do not practice her song
                            unpracticed
                                    as you are
        she has seen
                    so many lovers   bury each other
                                                    in grave dirt
                        you have no shovels
                                    with which to claw
                                            the earth

Brother Fool
        I warn you from marigolds   and white oleander
            I warn you   from chrysanthemums
                                                            or
you
will court the disease   you crave
                                    without antidote

Brother Fool
        there is no witch
                or wedding bed
                        or child born in a tulip
                                    for you to foster
        no daughter
            no son
                        only the house of belonging
                            you build yourself.

V

Mythology of the Restless

After Richard Siken

In the dreams I've told no one,
you lay your head in my lap,
and all the wolves fall silent.

Tether
After Samuel Ace

I was called back   into the streets   the sidewalk

      the cracked pavement   beneath boot   tasting the little hours

cooling chamomile   against haunted tea shops   the tequila nightclub crawl

      catching the lighting shimmer   of eyes in the neon,   oh bless

my gondola-cut canals   and parking lot hour talks

      the passion-tender kisses of friends   and strangers   blooming

in magnolia air how we held each other and bore the walking

      of the whole quiet world by moonshine   I was called back

by electric storms   of rain   the soaked bone laughter

      of my cobblestone dancing   the open throated song   of amethysts

glittering in a carnival   of swirling capes   and ombre tulle

      of hornsand the sunlight glitter   of golden bells

on ankles   shaking earthquakes   in the sweating honeysuckle heat

      of bare-breasted jazz   and bourbon   this crooked   open road

where I have been nothing   but alone.

The Gingerbread Cake

In his long fingers   the egg,
      cool, unfiltered as blue skies,   breaks
          its heart and drips
              a golden belly,
     slung low
          in cupped clay.

    I bear the ache of red feathers

                                   she'll say,
          lightning in her eyes,
with all the windburn,   of her blazing flight.

    I am a simple woman,
        and I hunger for a home.

At her arrival he shreds the sun
    with brown sugar,
               a divination
         cast in entrails   of sweetness,
     by the warmth
        of ancestral advice.
In his simmer, he melts
    the honey, the butter,
        the cinnamon,
    sprinkling ginger
          and cloves
            like the autumn
of her laughter,   an omen
    of lit hearth and brewed tea,
                    a portent
        of ripped sheets
           petalling around
        their spread   and spilling.
She watches him coil
    the marzipan,
         winking a village
           of language
    in the roll of his wrists,   *a home,*

she orders.
So he bakes her one,
        with apricot jam
                and chocolate buttercream.
He removes her scabbard,   unlaces
                her gauntlets,
        and calms her burning
                with a nest,
                        a nestle,
                                a cake
    to silence
                        the thunder.

The Hand That Controls Me

What controls me
rests upon my throat,
ready to rake rubies,
to twist the wind
into knots for sailing.
Is protection, knows
when to stop my voice
in a hangman's noose.

It has plucked grapes from the lips
of the hungry, has poured wine
into mouths of ancients,
twisted the lightning bolts
of storms into diamond strikes—
I shake at its presence,
I curl around its mercy

and the hand presses its palm
to my cheek. I am frightened
by its unscarred wrist,
Its strong nails, the way it knows
what to do to make me moan.

What voice need I
after it holds my tongue?

Reawakening

Let the flint spark of metal on metal
set fire to feathers long plucked from bone.
Wing as ash, wing as smoke, wing on a drowned
man, a talisman nailed to a barn door.
Tear up the floorboards, pull down the haystacks.
It is time to return to the spin of the world,
to the song and place of things,
to the presence that has been forgotten
and swept into the walls of a house breaking
in its heart. If dust has filled your teacup,
wipe it clean. Trust your hands and carve
new railings for the staircase. Spiral the wood,
find purpose in a pot of basil, a sprig of rosemary.
Let your ponds fill with moss.
Cook your fish on a river's edge.
Let the stars fill your wine cup,
and drink the moon in its reflection.
They have been waiting for you,
the birds, the snakes, the warbling trill
of new life in an eggshell.
Bury the bones of your lover
beneath a lemon tree.
Dig up the grave of your
bottled blood.
Drink back the veins you have spilled,
and invite yourself
to cross the threshold
of home.

Small Talk

There is nothing else in life
        worth breathing for
                but to share good bounty
                with the ones you love.

That,

                and orgasms.

Metaphors for My Body in Midwinter

I am cherished here, fed risengrød in appeasement,
in pleasure, for my hands, a hearth; my kiss, mistletoe.
My tongue is a dumb cake's silent ceremony,
and every dream that passes this frozen river,
wears a wreath of cherrywood and myrrh, cuts down
every illusion of helplessness with a birch switch.

I move as deer, as jackrabbit in hawkflight,
A red-breasted bird, a bonfire of oak and holly.
I harness the sky with a cinnamon broom.
I sweep away the blighted root, the sorrow choke.
I make a speech of suppertime, bring milk and almonds
enough to feed the beasts of every hollow.

With ornaments for eyes, I horse dance
on every threshold, demand a serving
of red mandarins, a sip of buttered rum.
Let me ring your home with bells and ribbons,
let me partake in the blessings of this house,
this communion, a shelter from the snow.

Coals in the Earth

it returns to me
     unbidden,   unexpected
        as a rusting wave.

     I am   unarmored
in the ruling passions
        of my regalia,
     a leather and carnelian
        split throat
           choker
    an iron crown
        flecked with
           obsidian

my body
       is no longer   skinless
no longer   exposed muscles
     parched ivory
        rippling
with the lengthening
       of my teeth

    no
I am more honest   than I
        have ever been
    on the attributes
       of my humanity
if only for
    this miasma of light
       the truth
    of my wounds
        my aching

yet you offer yourself
                a nourishment
      to my gentled
            nibbling   a kiss
on your earlobes
      your neck
            the fingertips
that scritch
      beneath   my chin
            behind   my ears
      the rounds   of my belly

knowing
           by my smiles

                        at last
    safe harbor

Self-Portrait as a Heart, Exploded

So tender, this rubble of meat
these miles of songs breathed out
like a sunset dirge. See how they flaunt
their purple vanities, waltzing
in uneven staccato across the horizon.

They grow hands to clasp in palpitation,
oh there are faces between the palms,
oh they are thousands of men dredged up
from the deep like a handful of shells,
moaning their melancholy in the desert.

Look at how the sun rises like a nectarine,
how the split star drips ambrosia
in marinade. These thousand-handed hearts
would lift their fruits to your lips,
each man a soft-skinned morsel,

each man a naked note played
in the symphony of the wet, panting animals
you have become. What a shame
you have embroidered your mouth
shut, that you will not take any more

in gluttony. You have found the love
you would leave other loves for.

Tea House

I build a home with you
with round outer walls like *qīng-huā*,
papercut butterflies perching
on the fragrant strawberries of *khokhloma*.

You make me want to folk art,
be a mouse in a hollowed gourd,
embroider red goddesses on the curtains,
wash laundry in a chain-link stream.

Our home will nestle in the earth
as a delftware teapot, its curving tower,
its paper screen windows dripping
a well-bucket of books into the garden.

There, peonies and chrysanthemums
shall shade the stone table where
we'll brew a jasmine morning
with a cauldron of darkest Oolong.

Love Is Not My Name

Sweetheart   is not my name
though I bear it willingly
its petals   its weight   as I bathe
in the warmth   of a thousand tongues
from a thousand fires   that flicker
in earth core molt   against brass kettles
boiling tea   in a snowstorm

Darling is not my name
yet I chop onions   on a wooden board
mince garlic   to feed the flashing oils
of my open-belly   hungers
How I savor   your simmered
nutmeg maple   with each caress
of fingers slipped   across my smile

Precious   is not my name
even when you call me   thus with lips
pressed beneath a downy hairline
soft   against my wine-warmed cheeks
amidst the dark berries   of unmarked countryside
where even the birds   dare not sing

And though it is what you call me   Love
is not my name   unless it is also yours

Terra Firma

Forgive the flights of this tethered Icarus,
the way I wheel from sun to sea
in cycles of scorched and drowned body.
I have ever been a child of air,
with smoked lungs full of stardust
screaming from another world.

The pines of you call from dark forests,
and your honeybees dance in the light.
I entwine chrysanthemums in my hair
as your fingers pass through it.
I have never been so good, so safe
in spite of my giggled squirming.

Would that I take the stairs
down to where roots dwell,
where mushrooms bloom in rings,
and moss makes a bed where
the two of us can rest.

The Last Reader

It is you, wind whistle,
bard of crow and stream,
you who take my ring
of words into your mouth
wherever you find it.

Bog dreamer, you swallow me
straight from sea glass bottle,
from gold-cracked bowl,
from the oil slick burning
of orchids on a silk screen.

Because you knit
a bone crochet with the flame
of a lightning strike,
the hearth smoke escapes
of my vanishing body.

Ash-eater, confetti connoisseur
of cremation, I am yours
to set fire to among
the blood-red maples
in your teacup.

It is to you I offer
my passing life, my cat-hiss heart,
this threadbare song,
all that remains of these sunken
sighs made words again.

About the Author

Ellen Webre is a biracial, first-generation Taiwanese-American writer and educator born in Hong Kong and raised in California. She has wondrous good fortune to be blessed with the company of extraordinary writers, artists, and filmmakers, receiving her first blessing from the muses by attending the Creative Writing Conservatory of the Orange County High School of the Arts. Her work has most recently been published in *FreezeRay Poetry*, *Sh!t Men Say to Me: A Poetry Anthology in Response to Toxic Masculinity*, *Dark Ink: A Poetry Anthology Inspired by Horror*, and *Voicemail Poems*. Ellen is an avid lover and supporter of the Southern Californian poetry community, currently acting as a social media marketing specialist and videographer for Moon Tide Press and Two Idiots Peddling Poetry.

Acknowledgements

"Almond Blossom" was originally published in 2018 by Voicemail Poems. It was published again in 2021, in Moon Tide Press' *Sh*t Men Say to Me: A Poetry Anthology in Response to Toxic Masculinity.*

"Brother Fool" was published in 2021 in Moon Tide Press' *Sh*t Men Say to Me: A Poetry Anthology in Response to Toxic Masculinity.*

"Teenagers Will Scream If You Love Them" was published in 2021 in Moon Tide Press' *Sh*t Men Say to Me: A Poetry Anthology in Response to Toxic Masculinity.*

"Metaphors for My Body in Midwinter" was originally published in 2021 in Spirited Muse Press' Anthology *The Spirit of Winter.*

"Of Moss and Kerosene" was originally published in Issue #20 of *FreezeRay Poetry.*

"Old Stomping Grounds" and "Softball Poem" borrow their beginning lines from "normal-horoscopes" by CT Kelly.

Thank You

Firstly, thank you to all my parents, whose unconditional love and support has given me the most exquisitely fortunate and wonderful life. Thank you to my beloved sisters who are the bread and stars of my heart, to my strong and resilient grandmothers, to my generous and loving aunt and uncles, to my cousins who share with me the best memories of my childhood. Thank you to my extended family, my step-family, and all my ancestors who have built such a glorious household for me to grow up in.

Wholehearted gratitude to the poetry communities of Orange County, Long Beach, and Los Angeles, most especially for Phil, Ben, and Steve of Two Idiots Peddling Poetry. I would not have become the person or poet I am today without discovering this reading and my dearest found family. Thank you to the sparkling spaces, staff, features, and open-mic performers of The Definitive Soapbox, Shout! The Open Mic, and Pondwater for sharing your splendid minds and voices. Thank you to my Creative Writing Conservatory teachers at Orange County School of the Arts for planting the seeds of my creativity.

Thank you to my Moon Tide Family and everyone who has helped me bring this book into being. I am so honored to be counted among the ranks of such luminous poets. I am so appreciative of Eric Morago for his guidance and being such a generous mentor and publisher. It has been such a privilege to have the care and attention of the extraordinary Sheila J. Sadr, HanaLena Fennel, and Dania Ayah Alkhouli whose encouragement, critiques, and advice have helped me polish this book. I cannot express how grateful I am to Amanda Le for creating my cover art. It is such a gift to be able to pair my work with something so beautiful.

To my dearest friends, everyone I have ever loved, and everyone who has loved me. Thank you for your stories and all your acts of tenderness. Thank you for sharing yourselves and receiving my affection. You all have filled my world with such uncountable joys. I would not be the person I am without you.

Also Available from Moon Tide Press

Instructions for an Animal Body, Kelly Gray (2021)
Head *V* Heart: New & Selected Poems, Rob Sturma (2021)
Sh!t Men Say to Me: A Poetry Anthology in Response to Toxic Masculinity (2021)
Flower Grand First, Gustavo Hernandez (2021)
Everything is Radiant Between the Hates, Rich Ferguson (2020)
When the Pain Starts: Poetry as Sequential Art, Alan Passman (2020)
This Place Could Be Haunted If I Didn't Believe in Love, Lincoln McElwee (2020)
Impossible Thirst, Kathryn de Lancellotti (2020)
Lullabies for End Times, Jennifer Bradpiece (2020)
Crabgrass World, Robin Axworthy (2020)
Contortionist Tongue, Dania Ayah Alkhouli (2020)
The only thing that makes sense is to grow, Scott Ferry (2020)
Dead Letter Box, Terri Niccum (2019)
Tea and Subtitles: Selected Poems 1999-2019, Michael Miller (2019)
At the Table of the Unknown, Alexandra Umlas (2019)
The Book of Rabbits, Vince Trimboli (2019)
Everything I Write Is a Love Song to the World, David McIntire (2019)
Letters to the Leader, HanaLena Fennel (2019)
Darwin's Garden, Lee Rossi (2019)
Dark Ink: A Poetry Anthology Inspired by Horror (2018)
Drop and Dazzle, Peggy Dobreer (2018)
Junkie Wife, Alexis Rhone Fancher (2018)
The Moon, My Lover, My Mother, & the Dog, Daniel McGinn (2018)
Lullaby of Teeth: An Anthology of Southern California Poetry (2017)
Angels in Seven, Michael Miller (2016)
A Likely Story, Robbi Nester (2014)
Embers on the Stairs, Ruth Bavetta (2014)
The Green of Sunset, John Brantingham (2013)
The Savagery of Bone, Timothy Matthew Perez (2013)
The Silence of Doorways, Sharon Venezio (2013)
Cosmos: An Anthology of Southern California Poetry (2012)
Straws and Shadows, Irena Praitis (2012)
In the Lake of Your Bones, Peggy Dobreer (2012)
I Was Building Up to Something, Susan Davis (2011)
Hopeless Cases, Michael Kramer (2011)
One World, Gail Newman (2011)

What We Ache For, Eric Morago (2010)
Now and Then, Lee Mallory (2009)
Pop Art: An Anthology of Southern California Poetry (2009)
In the Heaven of Never Before, Carine Topal (2008)
A Wild Region, Kate Buckley (2008)
Carving in Bone: An Anthology of Orange County Poetry (2007)
Kindness from a Dark God, Ben Trigg (2007)
A Thin Strand of Lights, Ricki Mandeville (2006)
Sleepyhead Assassins, Mindy Nettifee (2006)
Tide Pools: An Anthology of Orange County Poetry (2006)
Lost American Nights: Lyrics & Poems, Michael Ubaldini (2006)

Patrons

Moon Tide Press would like to thank the following people for their support in helping publish the finest poetry from the Southern California region. To sign up as a patron, visit www.moontidepress.com or send an email to publisher@moontidepress.com.

Anonymous
Robin Axworthy
Conner Brenner
Nicole Connolly
Bill Cushing
Susan Davis
Peggy Dobreer
Dennis Gowans
Alexis Rhone Fancher
Hanalena Fennel
Half Off Books & Brad T. Cox
Donna Hilbert
Jim & Vicky Hoggatt
Michael Kramer
Ron Koertge & Bianca Richards
Gary Jacobelly
Ray & Christi Lacoste
Zachary & Tammy Locklin
Lincoln McElwee
David McIntire
José Enrique Medina
Michael Miller & Rachanee Srisavasdi
Michelle & Robert Miller
Ronny & Richard Morago
Terri Niccum
Andrew November
Jeremy Ra
Luke & Mia Salazar
Jennifer Smith
Andrew Turner
Rex Wilder
Mariano Zaro
Wes Bryan Zwick

Made in the USA
Columbia, SC
11 February 2023

11466596R00067